SYNODIC

INTIMACY

MONTARIO HAMPTON

Lanico Media House

Celebrating literary lessons and legacies

TEXAS • ARKANSAS • LOUISIANA

SYNODIC INTIMACY

Copyright © 2018 Montario Hampton

Lanico Media House is an imprint of Lanico Enterprise.

Lanico Media House

ISBN: 978-0-9986520-6-1

First Printing 2018, Printed in the United States.

For those who are still trying to understand love.
Enjoy the journey of discovery.

Introduction

The moon is an ancient and trusted symbol of cycles. It is constant, reliable, and also mystical. It affects gravity, tides and even fertility. The power and magic of the moon has spawned many tales, theories and mystical books, all with the hope to shed a little light on the phases of the moon and with it, life itself.

I discovered by happenstance that relationships are a lot like the phases of the moon. They rotate on an axis of meet, desire, love, and unfortunately too often, loss. Then the cycle starts again until it is interrupted or changed somehow. The rotation of a celestial body in relation to another body is called a synodic cycle. How befitting when you look at the rotations we make with each other's heart and soul.

This book is poetry and principle meshed together to help you see the truth of who you are in the midst of relating to others, to your significant others. Maybe this book will save a few relationships. Maybe it will inspire new ones. Maybe it will end some. But it will definitely affect you, and if you allow it, teach you how to maintain no matter if the moon is at full power in your life or you are currently on the waning side of life and love.

New Love

New Beginnings

Six months had passed and still I held on to the pain
How could she, after I had given her everything
I couldn't help but feel like maybe I was to blame

I stood faithfully for two years
Only to see my fiancé give birth to another man's child
The news brought me to tears

But I soon discovered everything has a purpose
As one door shuts another one opens
Through which, for me, walked a woman truly worth it

She was everything I thought I had lost
And everything that I knew I was missing
Though this union came at a high cost

I was thankful to the Most High
For saving me from living a lie
And possibly raising a child that wasn't even mine

I have found love in my heart once more

Dear Beautiful

Because I'm shy, I decided to write you a note
Every time I see you, your beauty causes my heart to slow
Anyone would be lucky to have a woman like you
Unique, humble, radiant, & intelligent too
Truthfully, I've had my eyes on you for a while
I know I'm not your type, but I'm sure I can make you smile
Financially & physically you're out of my league, but
Unlike the others, emotionally & physically, I can keep you intrigued
Love the IT Guy, Steve.

Ms. Rain

Today I received a message from a beautiful young lady
I opened it, wasn't expecting hearts & smiles
We talked; we should definitely meet one day, maybe
Her conversation was worth me traveling 100 miles

She was more radiant than I expected
Never imagined meeting someone so humble & beautiful
So intelligent & very self-respected
She came home with me & never wanted to leave.
The feeling was mutual

Coffee Shop

I come to the coffee shop every day
And every day I see her beautiful face
And every day I fail to formulate the words to say

I come to the coffee shop every day to look in her eyes
In her eyes I see a humble woman full of pride
And in her eyes I see a strong woman passed all the pain she hides

Today I came to the coffee shop with one intention
The intention to bring desires to fruition
To ask her to be my woman and wait for a decision

Growing Affection

There was always something about you
I'm unsure what it was
Maybe it was just a crush

I felt like we were similar
Even though our differences caused tension
Plus you were taken, not to mention
So being with you was never my intention

But sometimes love is found in strange places
Our disparities were replaced by friendship
My infatuation for you became endless
Your inner beauty had captured my full attention
One day you will be mine, hope I don't sound pretentious

Chance

The first day I saw her was her first day at the company
We'd had many employees come and go, none quite so beautiful
I was married, I reminded myself constantly
But my boss assigned her to me for training ironically

Once her training was complete, I was promoted
I agreed to transfer for double my original salary
After my transfer, I was told my salary was misquoted
I left the company and shortly thereafter had marital problems

Who could have known four years later our paths would cross again
She had crossed my mind several times, now here we stand face to face
We became reacquainted and I began to desire her as more than just a friend
Here's the opportunity to pursue what I never had the chance to

ATL

Following a promotion, I decided to tour with the CMO
Our first stop was in GA to unveil new products
During our initial conference, I met a beautiful black queen
She was VP of Marketing for a sister company and assigned to my team

After the conference, we went out for drinks
We became very acquainted as we discussed marketing strategies
Never had I met a woman so beautiful and intelligent
The more she talked, the more mesmerized I became by her elegance

Internal dating wasn't recommended; we didn't care
We found something in one another that we never had before
She said she was never letting go and I was truly convinced
Because for the first time in my life, my heart was truly content

Covet

Never covet another man's wife
Yet here I am
My heart seeking after her
And me not giving a damn

A woman beautiful in every way
Seeking only to be appreciated
And a husband with no honor
Only leaving her humiliated

She deserves more
And one day she'll see that
When that day comes
I pray for the opportunity to be that

Goddess

A Goddess amongst women
I stare into her eyes, therein lies divinity
Her gaze penetrates the depths of my soul
As if the universe stands still in awe of her brilliancy

Who is she? My heart longs to know
As I struggle to escape her mesmerizing allure
I begin to fantasize as if I was trapped in a hypnotic state
My thoughts becoming impure

Who is she? I have to know
An appearance so exquisite yet a demeanor so modest
I opened my mouth but was unable to speak
Someone tell me please, who is this Goddess?

Waxing Love

Howling At The Moon

You're a crazy chick
That's what I love about you
We have so much fun
There's nothing together we can't do

Last night we walked
You were humming a tune
I had the idea
Let's howl at the moon

You laughed at me first
Then threw back your head
The moon was full
Your lips were red

We hooted and hollered awhile
I could only smile
Who would have thought we'd be howling at the moon

What I Feel

When you're not around
I miss you so
Even through our ups and downs
I'll never let you go

No one can ever take your place
You're the only one for me
The feeling I get when looking at your face
Let me know I want this to be

You're everything to me, my world
Hopefully one day my wife
I love you dearly, you're the only girl
I want forever in my life

Silence of the Mind

I suppose life without you
Would be life not so true
For my dream is to be with you
And I won't stop until that dream comes true

They say one man's trash is another man's treasure
And to be with you I would go to any measure
I guess that truly makes you this man's treasure
And nothing else could ever measure

For as much as I do say there's much left unsaid
Things I don't say and just let roam through my head
The things that I don't say are better left unsaid
Because words can't describe what goes through my head

Uncertainty

Any given moment could be our very last
No one knows when their time will come to pass
Some hope and they pray, some joke and they play
But few consider this could be their last day

Life and its problems come and go just as the wind blows
It's full of uncertainties but before my body turns cold
I want you to know as sure as the sky is blue
That I truly love you

Know

Know what you mean to me
Know how much I really care
Know that nothing could ever separate us
Not a love so rare

Know how I feel
Know of my love for you
Know that no matter what happens
I'll always be there to see you through

Who

Who could ever love you the way I do?
A love departed not so soon
One never spoken mildly of
Outlasting the stars and the moon

Who could continuously stand by your side?
Enduring hardships and wind
Never removed by them
There until the very end

Who would surely give their all?
In the drop of a dime
Never waived by doubt
There until the end of time
Who?

Love Undefined

There's no way to say
how or what I feel.
Saying I love you
doesn't cover the whole bill.

Love is only a four-letter word
until true meaning is defined,
made clear, and understood;
It'll always be a repeated line

When I say I love you,
I mean it from the bottom of my heart.
I'll never let you go,
even when times get hard.
Baby I love you.

It's Yours

The way you make me feel
Can be defined as unreal
Your love softened a hardened heart
Your love sometimes makes me just fall apart

You're not just another pretty face
You're someone that can't be replaced
I'm giving you my heart, now what will you do
All I ask is be careful whatever you choose

My heart is in your hands
I'm here at your demand
Stay forever true to me
And we will always be

Here

Here I stand
And here will I remain
By your side
And that will never change

Here I am
And here I will always stand
By your side
Like no other can

First Yearning

Shower

Today was a hot summer day
I enjoy you, I'm glad you decided to come back to my place
We've been out in this Louisiana heat for hours
Yet it still caught me off guard when you grasped my hand & said
"Let's take a shower."

This was my first time seeing you undressed
Damn woman, I'm impressed!
Watching this hot water drip down your breast,
has me at alert. You grabbed it and began to caress.

Your kiss is so passionate
You softly grip it and grab it
You just don't know how bad I want you
I pulled you closer, we can do whatever you want to.

Who Has To Know

For quite a while, I've known you
We became very close over the course of time
You were off limits, yet we still became intimate
Contrary to everyone's knowledge, you were mine

Who has to know how often I visit you at work
Who has to know I'm the reason you always wear a skirt
At your job in the ladies' restroom
At your parents' house in the guest bedroom

I know we shouldn't but it feels every bit of right.
The warmth of your mouth every night when we're at a red light
I pull out of traffic just so I can feel you
No one had to know, just know I feel so alive when I feel you

Office

Another late night at the office
Not tonight
She works late often
But tonight is my night
She looked surprised
to see me
As I looked in her eyes
and whispered "Shut the door please,
I'm not here to talk.
Come here"
I bit my lip as she walked
"How long have you been here?"
She looked at me and asked
as I bit her ear
and grabbed her ass.
"Shhh" I said
"Take off your clothes
but leave the heels"
I kissed her neck as I gripped her throat
"How does it feel" I asked
As she laid on her desk. I began sucking her clit
"Tonight dinner was promised to me
or did you forget?" I asked
Nevertheless it was a promise I made her keep

Kiss

When we kissed, my soul burned with passion
She pulled my hair as she kissed my neck
And then she unbuckled my pants
As my heart began to pound in my chest

She began to unbutton my shirt
I could feel her kisses getting lower and lower
Her mouth felt so warm as she wrapped it around me
How could I not want more and more?

She climbed on top of me
I slowly pushed every inch in
She screamed as she looked in my eyes and then kissed me
And I came inside of her as we were kissing

Burning Fantasy

Around you the fire becomes intense
Your smell, your touch, your kiss draws me from within
Causing flames increasingly hot until my clothes become a vent
Off shall they go, enough time has been spent

Your body is soft just as your smell
Your kiss is moist just as yourself
Your temperature is warm; your love as well
At the end of the night, it all seemed as a fantasy tale

Tonight

Walk in this room
Forget everyone else
They don't matter
I just want you to enjoy yourself

Lay on this bed
Hold my body tight
Don't let go
We're in for a long night

Relax your body
I see you're tense
Let me undress you
Enough suspense

Time seems slow
Your body is getting warmer
Minutes are becoming like hours
I'm nothing like your former

The night is coming to an end
Your body feels right
Your head seems light
How will you ever forget such a night?

First Time

We began undressing before we made it to the door
I kissed you so aggressively, you nearly collapsed to the floor
I pushed you against the wall, I've been waiting for this
I looked in your eyes as we kissed and rubbed my fingers across your clit
You wrapped your legs around my waist
As I entered your sacred place
You dug your nails into my back
It felt so good yet it hurt so bad
The deeper your nails went, the deeper I went
I put my arms under your legs, now you feel every inch
You went from moaning to screaming my name
I whispered in your ear *I love you,* you wrapped your arms around me
and I didn't stop until we both came

Fellatio

Laying here looking in your eyes while you shove it in your throat
It's a lot baby, try not to choke
You circle your tongue around the tip
And stroke the base with such a soft grip
You're so beautiful, and your mouth so warm
You take it out your mouth and lick up the slightly curved form
You began to stroke it and smile, you looked impressed
You kept going until I climaxed and you didn't leave a mess

Desire

Thoughts turn into desires
Those desires into needs
Douse this eternal fire
As I penetrate you ever so deep

I can feel you begin to stretch
As I push forward
You wrap your hand around my neck
And whisper, "Daddy I want more"
I look into your eyes
As the strokes become harder
I can feel the trembling in your thighs
As I push in further
"Please don't stop daddy"
I hear as your heart begins pacing
I won't baby
Not until I fulfill your inner most craving

Waxing Promise

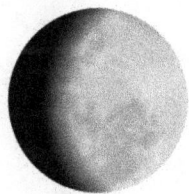

Silence of the Heart

We don't have to exchange words
And often times we don't
Through eye contact alone
I can read your every thought

They gaze upon your beauty
And their hearts are filled with desire
As I gaze upon your soul
My heart is consumed fire

And when I enter your body
It's as if the universe is converging
Our bodies become one
As our souls are emerging

We don't have to exchange words
We can just stare into each other's eyes
And through eye contact alone
Our hearts' desires can be realized

A Rare Love

Never in my days have I met anyone like you
Never have I felt a love like yours
A love true through and through

Just the very sound of your voice brightens my day
The thought of your love brings tears to my eyes
Only if you knew the joy I felt inside

A day without you in my world,
Is a day without the sun on Earth
And a day I come to more appreciate your worth

Cater To Her

"Come hit this & ease your mind while I rub your feet
How was your day? Is there anything you need?
Want me to run you some bath water or cook you something to eat?"
I asked as I gently kissed her feet
"The bath water sounds nice", she replied
I can see the glaze in her eyes
I ran her some bath water and lit some candles
She walked in the bathroom, I pulled her closer by her love handles
She's a chubby girl, but I love it
She's beautiful, amazing, and lovely
As I stand here and look her in her eyes, I know I want to
spend the rest of my life with her
I'll make her my Misses and I'll be her Mister

Woman of My Dreams

Without you where would I be?
You opened up my heart, allowed me to see
By your side, no other place I'd rather be

My love stretched as a sea
To meet your any and every need
With a woman in which I am so pleased
With the thought of kneeling my knees

From my heart you will never leave
From my mind you will never flee
The day I stood by your side so it seemed
That I would always be standing by the woman of my dreams

Belle

My heart cries your name
In your eyes, I can see the pain
And I can see the distrust and the fear
The fear that just like them, I'll disappear

But in my eyes, what do you see?
Do you see love, passion, loyalty?
Do you see the pain and frustration of my past?
Or do you simply see another man like the last?

I see a woman worth holding on to
A woman that makes it worth all I've been through
So cry your tears and allow me to wipe them from your face
Because I promise you, I'm here to stay
I love you Belle

Love's Prison

Your attentiveness
and your beauty captures me
How do I break free?

I don't nor should I
Rather let me cling to you
and sing thy heart's truth

For if love's a prison,
freedom is a form of hell
Take the key to my cell

Falling

When I close my eyes, I see your face so clearly
Your eyes, your smile, you're such a beauty
You run through my mind constantly
Yet you suffer no exhaustion from all the running
Why can't I stop fantasizing about you?
When I'm not with you, I'm unsure what to do
Wanting to be with you is the only thing I'm sure of
Guess I truly am falling in love

The Way I See Her

She can be hard to deal with
From her attitude to her aggressive demeanor
The jealousy and the paranoia
Because she doesn't want anything to come between us
You may never see her the way that I do
You may never understand why I choose to stay by her side
You may look at her and see a damaged woman
But all I see is unconditional love when I look into her eyes
You can't comprehend what we have
Nor are you meant to
What we have is for us
That's why you'll never see her the way that I do

With You

Within weeks of knowing you
I wanted to spend the rest of my life with you
You became my best friend; hopefully one day my wife
You motivated me and brought joy into my life

The day we met, happiness flooded my world
My life without you would be similar to a pearl necklace without the pearls
I'm ready to move forward and make you my wife
Because I'm certain that it's with you that I want to spend the rest of my life

Full Commitment

Day In The Sun

You've been good to me
I can't complain
So today is your day
To alleviate the strain

I'm running your bath
I'm cooking your food
I'm changing the diapers
Anything to lighten your mood

You can sit and relax
Listen to a song or two
Get a pedicure
Anything you want to do

For your sweetness
The peace and all the fun
For your generosity
This is your day in the sun

A Quiet Tear

I had to work late tonight
I tipped in the door at 1 am
You were laying there fast asleep
My firstborn son cradled to you sleeping too

I stood there transfixed
It was like I was under a spell
My perfect wife gave me a perfect son
Both asleep in my bed

I looked around the house
We weren't rich but well-fed
I think about how little you ask for
Stuff like that makes me want to hustle more

My right cheek was damp
I don't even know when it happened
But looking at and loving my family
I guess a quiet tear slipped into the dark

Promise To Keep

Washing, vacuuming, doing the dishes
Cooking up a master plan
Gotta fulfill her wishes

I promised her if she stuck it out
Though now we walk
We'll have some clout

We live under the shadow with a friend
But you can believe your man
These days will end

Right now I know she's fast asleep
I'm out here for her
I have a promise to keep

Better Things

Even when they don't
Things always change
What was once out of reach
Is now within range

You took me at a promise
You never asked for anything
You were easy to please
That's why you got the ring

It's an apartment and a Pontiac
That's what you currently see
It'll be a BMW and a home
Just work with me
I'm going to give you better things

Holding Your Hand

I held your hand on our first date
We hung out all day and stayed up late
I held your hand in the mall
I was holding it when I began to fall
The first time I said I do
I was holding your hand, looking at you
The first contraction with my son
I knew I'd hold your hand over the long run
There are those days when I want to let go
But just the thought hurts me so
This will end like it all began
With me being your husband, holding your hand

Daddy Coming

I was getting ready for work
You climbed up on my leg
You looked up at me
Like your eyes would beg

My firstborn son
It is always hard to leave you
I pick you up for a brief second
I hug and kiss you

I heard you call for me
It was late last night
Daddy is coming, son
I got you whether you're wrong or right

MMM

I want to dedicate these next three poems to my three sons. Kids are a very important piece when it comes to family and relationships. And most of the time when a relationship fails and a family is broken apart, it's the kids that suffer the most. I can speak from experience because I have watched my sons be affected by the relationships I had with their mothers.

Montario Jr, Marquis, & Mason I want you to know that daddy loves you. And though at the time I wrote this y'all were too young to read, I hope that one day you do read it and know in your hearts that daddy does and has always loved all three of you. And I always will.

Jr.

Tonight your mother just gave me some news I've been waiting years
to hear
Her test was positive this time which mean you're finally on your way
here
I was instantly proud
I've been awaiting your arrival for some time now.
You don't know me yet, but soon you'll learn my voice.
You're my first child, so be patient with me on this new course
I'll do my best because you're the best I've ever had
Someday I'll call you Jr & you'll call me dad.
I love you

Marquis

You came at an unexpected time
but I looked forward to your arrival
You would be the second son of mine
and I was so excited
You came out looking like your brother
But you grew into your own
Now you look more like your mother
But you'll always be daddy's baby
I love you

Mason

I feel like I failed your older brothers
Especially the oldest, we were the closest
He didn't respond well to the separation of me & his mother
I learned from that mistake, I gain strength when I see your face
When you were born, it felt like my second chance
You were so cute, to your mom I salute
I fell in love at first glance
Daddy's just letting you know, Daddy will never let you go
I love you

Waning Affection

Accidents

My life almost escaped me today
When I found out my family was nearly taken away
All my dreams virtually came to an end
After you left the house with a friend
A car accident opened my eyes
The report of a wreck came as a surprise
I rushed to the hospital to your side
At that point I was done with pride
Seeing you and my sons in pain
Weighed heavily upon my brain
I began rethinking what made me mad
My past mistakes were making me sad
Accidents happen all the time
Life has no rhythm or rhyme
But I'll never take for granted future days
From now on I'll be a husband who prays

I Love You Still

We laid together wondering where we went wrong
Trying to pick up the pieces, where has the time gone?
This was one of our more peaceful moments
A moment of reconciliation & atonements

I look in your eyes and remember why I fell for you
I want to apologize for everything I've put you through
I realize now this relationship deserves another chance
Let's take our time and make new plans

There are promises I want to keep
Truth we both need to speak
A relationship that declined after its peak
A new path our hearts seek
I love you still.

Dying Star

Somehow we managed to survive the worst of it
But yet I can feel the fire inside dying
Despite the determination and perseverance
The struggle and hardship has us divided

The only laughter we share now is in memory
The star that burns the fastest usually burns the brightest
The way your eyes used to burn with passion
Those same eyes are now lifeless

I hope you accept, I truly apologize
There's so much more I could've done better
But I plan on honoring my vows
And I will do everything I can to pull this marriage back together
May our light burn bright once more

Insecurity

Would you believe me if I told you she was just a friend?
You're more focused on making me your problem rather than fixing
your own.
Everything that doesn't go your way is a sin.
Tell when was the last time you paid attention to anything other than
your phone?

If you don't do your job, how is that my issue?
She shows me the attention you fail to.
Hard to miss what you never had yet I miss you.
And by the way, every attempt she ever made fell through.

DAMN!

We began with laughter and lots of smiles
Talking on the phone for hours
Driving over hundreds of miles

We just clicked
Or so I thought
I was sure
You were the one I'd sought

But now the sound of your voice irk my nerve
I cannot love you as you deserve
You will not do the simplest things for me
Not one of my points can you see

I want it to be over
Finished, we're done
I was about to call it quits
But we found out you were pregnant with my son

DAMN!

Dilemma

I sit here and stare at my son wondering is it all worth it
He's a beautiful baby boy, looks just like you
Together y'all make the most beautiful family I could imagine

Yet I sit up at night hurting
I should have taken more time to think this through
But I never thought this would happen

Now I rarely ever smile after soul searching
Nothing but misery where the love once grew
How do I choose between my family and my own happiness?

She Was...

I didn't expect to fall
I didn't know I was weak
I was standing tall
Then came my losing streak

She was kind
Attentive to my needs
The kind that's hard to find
Like a flower among weeds

At home was no peace
But she was my fun
She provided sweet release
From the complainer who made me want to run

Still I feel bad
I know I'm better than this
She was something I'd never had
I guess it was something I could miss

Balance It Out

Emotions
Throwing a monkey wrench in my marriage
No peace at home
And she's always blowing up my phone

Postpartum depression
That excuse to be unreasonable
She's always complaining or mean
It's like a middle child wanting to be seen

Mad about wind
What can I do about it?
Tripping over problems as I come through the door
All my dreams shattered on the floor

My Body Lays Here

My body lays here next to yours
I hear you talking and I respond but I am not listening
Why am I even here with you?
Our home is nothing more than my own personal prison

My body may lay here next to yours
But my heart has long escaped your grasp
All the complaining and you have it easy
Surrounded by strong, intelligent women and you struggle with the
simplest task

Although my body lays here next to yours today
There will come a day full of regret
A day you'll wish that you paid attention
A day another woman will have earned my love and respect

Last Apology

Hard Time

Times had gotten hard
Even though I had mine, you had lost your job
Not to mention child support
Hearings, proceedings, in and out of court
The back pay and the fact your unemployment was denied
I could no longer ignore the tears you cried
It was time to do whatever it took
I took the rest of my money to Martinez and got what I could
A year later most of our problems were solved
Another year passed and I still was involved
It was time to get out but I was blinded
You warned me, but your words, I undermined
Who knew I was being investigated
I left to go to the store but never made it
I sit in this cell writing this letter to you
Begging your forgiveness and these next ten years you see me through
I love you

When I Finally Do

I'm leaving you one day
You better learn to pray
I will not be miserable with you
Better things I could do
I'm not your punching bag
You went from hot to hag
Dream girl is now a nightmare
To the point I no longer care

It's going to end, I swear
Give up quick, I don't dare
But you're going to feel it when I finally do
I'll show you the meaning of through

Complaints

I wasn't in the door well
You began nagging and raising hell
It would be nice if a meal was prepared
How did my day go? It would be nice if you actually cared

Never mind the work related incident that could have claimed my life
I'll sit here and listen to you remind me why I regret making you my wife
After a few moments, the sound of your voice grows faint
I no longer care to hear your complaints

This Is Goodbye

Many people say many things
Make promises they can't keep
But the day I say I'm done
I know you're going to weep

I know what I bring to the table
I'm a damn good man
I don't ask for much
Just need you to stick to the plan

I don't ask you to be perfect
I ask only that you try
If you can't even do that
Then baby, this is goodbye

Caught

My first thought was to kill you
Twelve hours a day, a five bedroom house, and a Benz
How dare you
I bust my ass and you say he's just a friend?
You say I'm just paranoid
I gave you the benefit of a doubt
My coworker hit a gas line
We were sent home early, that's the only reason I found out

Your Best Friend

Another night you have to work late
Another girls' night with your best friend
Another lie to my face
I let it slide so long you started making stupid mistakes

Too much bull shit and too many lies
He caused you to stop paying attention to what was important
You wasn't a friend, your husband was without a wife
But soon you would open your eyes

Your best friend showed up at our door step looking for you
You told me you were with her; she dropped her head
She told me everything you do
Can you really be mad that you walked in on us two?

Last Straw

Why are you really here
Am I just convenient
Do you really love me, or am I just an achievement

I've made numerous sacrifices
You took them for granted
But when I say I'm leaving, you always panic

You would like to stay
But do you want peace
Or are you just here to make sure you have a stable place to sleep

Your time is as short
as my patience is thin
The next time I walk out that door, I'm never coming back again

Assumptions

Assuming everything but responsibility for your actions,
how naïve and immature
The accusations and the finger pointing,
something I'm tired of having to endure

You assume because you're insecure
You're insecure due to you own shortcomings
You could listen, but you choose not to
Yet I'm to blame for the separation that is forthcoming

Bitterness

I feel the bitterness creeping in
I never imagined this day would come
The way I felt for you is hard to describe
But nowadays I hate to come home

You're beautiful without a doubt
The first time I saw you, my heart burned with desire
Your presence alone ignited passion
Now I sit here wondering what happened to that fire

I was prepared to give my life to you
Even decided not to pursue reconciliation with my wife for you
In you I thought I had found all that I longed for
Maybe I wouldn't have made that mistake if I knew the truth

Lie after lie, I uncovered as my heart shattered
I appeared crude but really my heart was weeping
It's been three years and now I realized you never really loved me
I've let the bitterness creep in

Waning Love

Broken Man

Standing at the blinds
How long have I been here
Our love boggled minds
Until you succumbed to fear

Questions about my past
Fears in every interaction
Wearing my nerve down to the last
Killing my attraction

Don't like being in the streets
But hate being at home
Don't want to be under her sheets
It's pain in my dome

I'm becoming what I hate
Breaking all I swore to you
You want to change? It's too late
This is what you've forced me to do

Great Act

Do you try to understand what isn't understood?
You act as you wish but never as you should
Is love and the fear of isolation but one concept in your mind?
You profess your love but your actions leave it undefined
Words of no meaning are words of no good

You create an illusion of depth but have less depth than a shallow grave
As an emotional sorcerer you create chaos and expect to escape unscathed
I plant seeds of wisdom in a barren mind
And pray they take root in time
But I'm left without a harvest of any kind, much to my dismay

In a great act of love for you, bonds must be broken
In an even greater act of love for myself, truth must be spoken
It's time for me to pick up the pieces and move forward
And cut all ties of discord
I send my regards; may God be with me on this new path I've chosen

I'll Love You Always

Has a thought ever brought you to your knees?
The thought that you may one day leave
The thought of you giving yourself to someone other than me
The fear that one day these thoughts could become reality

Today was the day that fear came true
You're really leaving after all we've been through
You said I knew one day this is what it would come to
And you were right but that doesn't mean I'll ever stop loving you

Finding Myself

Son. Man. Husband. Father.
I did it all right
But why did I bother?

Sitting here alone
Nothing but time to ponder
Looking at the picture
I can't help but wonder

But those little boys are my life
The only reason I can never regret making you my wife

But losing you, I lost a little of me
Fighting to hold on, but you wouldn't let it be
Checking on my own mistake
Laying here all night wide awake

I'm lost in the pain of the break
But searching for myself for the kids' sake

Final Day

This relationship has become a void
You can no longer listen to me without becoming annoyed
Therefore I'm no longer yours

Together we have become stagnant & I seek growth
I'm ambitious & seek for us both
But you're lazy in nature & do nothing but break oaths

Never wanted this to end in such a way
I'm done begging, I have nothing left to say
And even though I love you, this is our final day.

Last Night

Last night I slept alone
I told you to pack your things and go home
You packed your things and now you were gone

Last night was a terrible night
I took for granted the woman I wanted to make my wife
In this dark world, I lost my brightest light

Last night is one that I regret
I told you I regret the day we ever met
But honestly I regret the night you ever left

It's Over

We both know it's over, I'm just the first to admit it
I realize that without you, my world will keep spinning
You have been a hindrance and a distraction
I make a request, you take no action

I cook, I clean, I work
And in return, just heart break and hurt
You lay in bed and watch TV all day
You won't even get off your ass to clean your son's face

You expect me to stay in a relationship by myself
A relationship with no standards and no help
I would die before making you my wife
I'm moving on in search of a new life

Here's Your Key

Here's your key back
Why prolong the inevitable
What we had may never be replaceable
But what we had was also unsustainable
Pain & happiness intertwined with addiction & passion
Your love had become a drug, your presence a craving
Your touch took my breath but left my heart racing
When I began to drown in life, your voice was lifesaving
How do you let go of your heart without dying
Let go of your happiness without crying
I don't want to live without you is what I'm implying
But it's hard to please you, and I'm tired of trying.
So here's your key back.

Reckless

I woke up this morning
tears flowing.
I loved her
I wish I could hug her
one last time.
I miss walking up on her from behind
I miss hearing her laugh
sitting in the tub together taking baths.
She was my one
The mother of my son
Now my world is without a sun
because a drunk driver wanted to have fun.

About the Author

Poet, music lover, and mystic, Montario Hampton was born in Warren, AR and transplanted to Monroe, LA where he fell in love with word play and music. He works tirelessly on his mystical craft while encouraging others to pursue their dreams.

He is the store manager of Magickal Mystic and divides his time between being there and working at Xfinity where he has several times been named "Tech of the Month." Father to three little kings, Montario is always looking for ways to grow his legacy.

www.ingramcontent.com/pod-product-compliance
Lightning Source LLC
Chambersburg PA
CBHW062006040426
42447CB00010B/1934